ALFRED's

SACRED PERFORMER

COLLECTIONS

Late Int~~~

What Can I Play o~
Book 2: March & April Services

Arranged by Cindy Berry

10 Easily Prepared Piano Arrangements for March & April Services

Have you ever thought, "I wish I had *one* piano book that included appropriate hymn arrangements for the next couple of months"? As a church accompanist, I have shared that thought with you! *What Can I Play on Sunday?* is a series of six books, each book containing easily prepared pieces that are appropriate for a two-month period of the year. Book 1 is for January and February, Book 2 for March and April, and so on. Each book serves as a wonderful resource for your worship-planning needs for each season of the year. If your church uses Lectionary-based worship, these arrangements should be appropriate for those needs as well.

Book 2 contains arrangements that are especially appropriate for the months of March and April, and includes selections for Lent, Palm Sunday, Holy Thursday/Communion, Good Friday and Easter, as well as several general hymns. The other books in this series are as follows:

Book 1: January and February
Book 3: May and June
Book 4: July and August
Book 5: September and October
Book 6: November and December

I pray that you will find this series useful as you play your praises to God on Sundays, or use these arrangements for your own personal worship times.

Cindy Berry

Alfred

SAVIOR, LIKE A SHEPHERD LEAD US WITH
HE LEADETH ME

William Bradbury
Arr. Cindy Berry

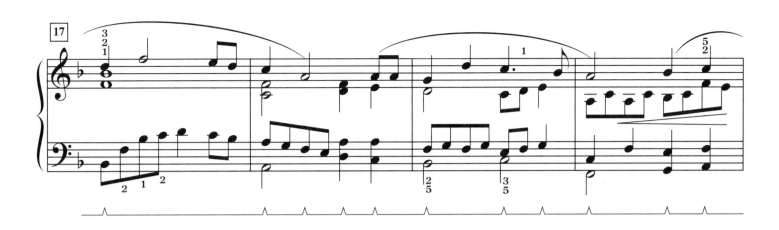

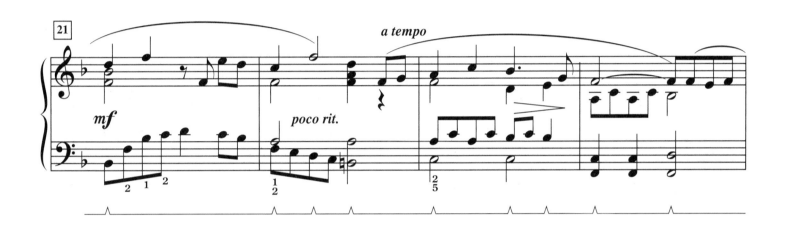

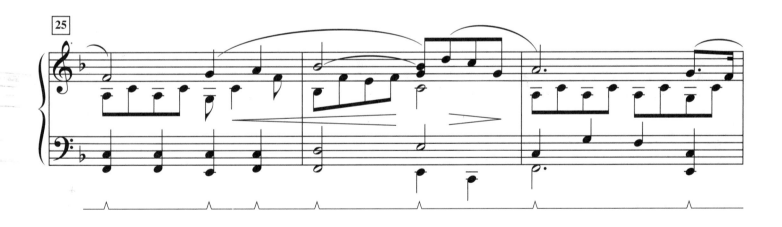

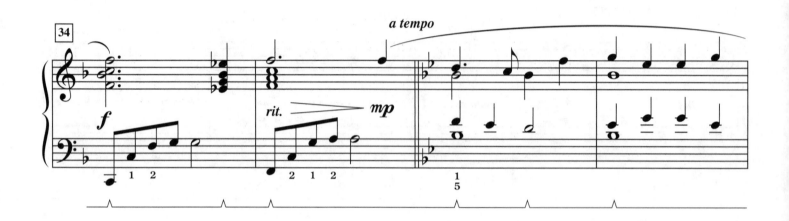

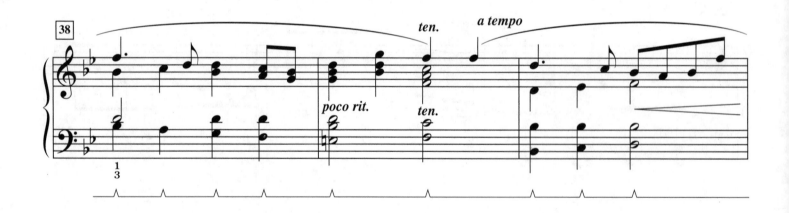

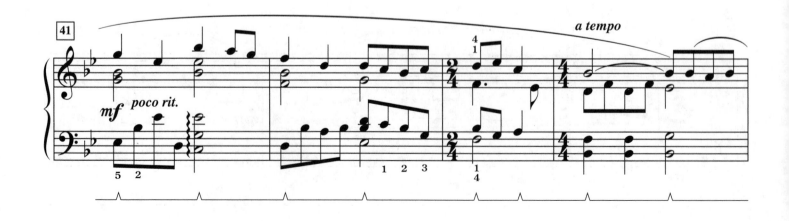

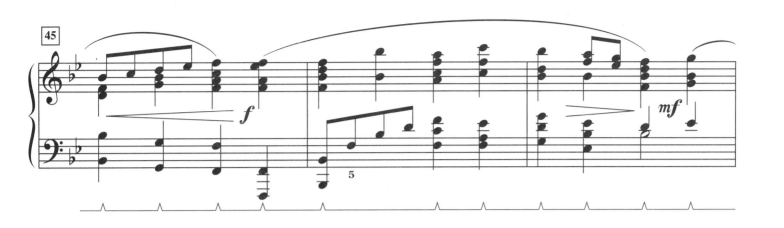

ALL GLORY, LAUD AND HONOR

Melchior Teschner
Arr. Cindy Berry

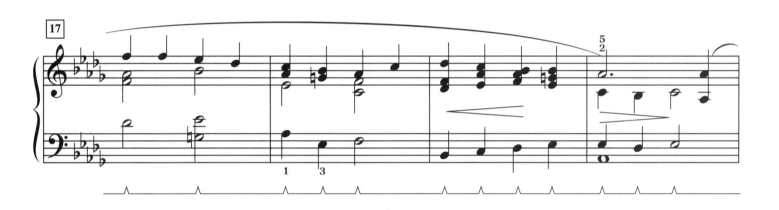

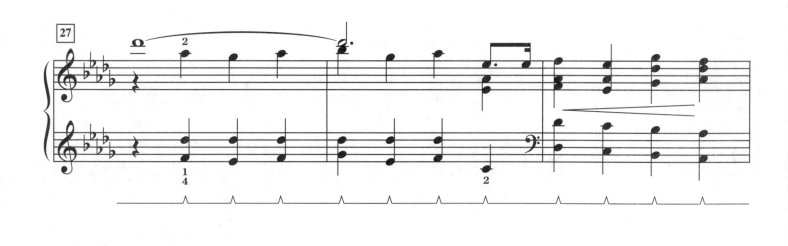

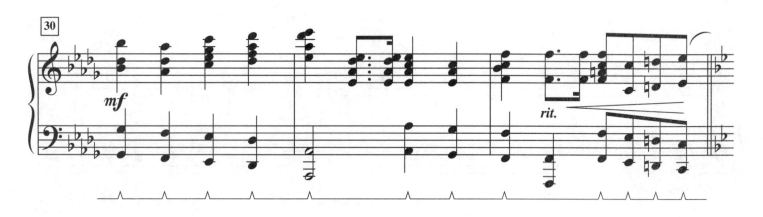

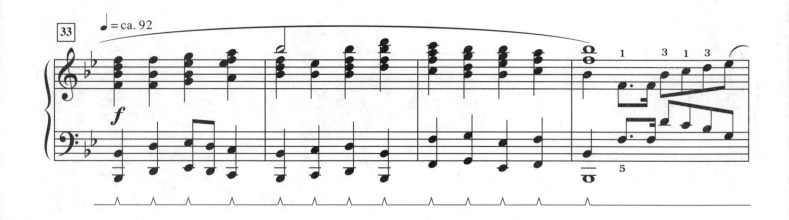

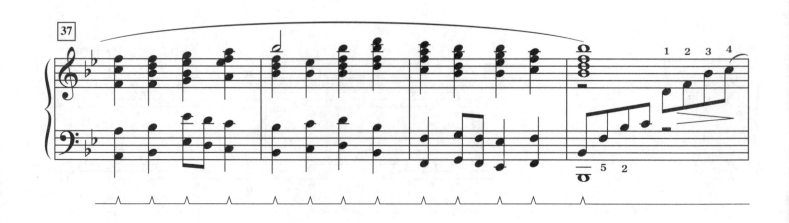

LIFT HIGH THE CROSS

Sydney H. Nicholson
Arr. Cindy Berry

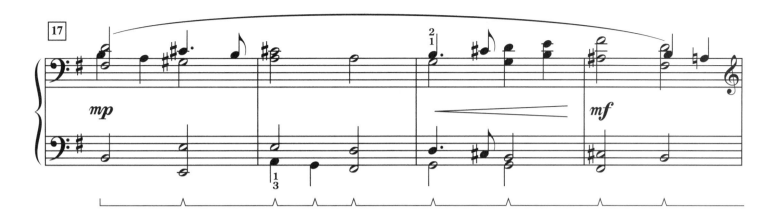

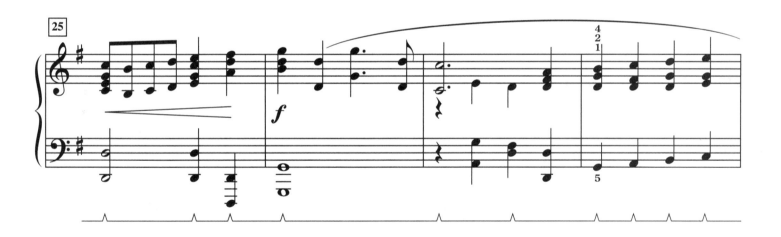

LET US BREAK BREAD TOGETHER

Spiritual
Arr. Cindy Berry

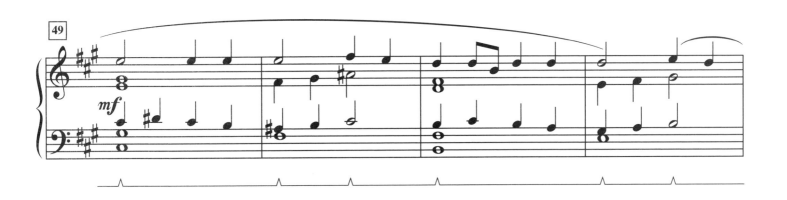

WERE YOU THERE?

Spiritual
Arr. Cindy Berry

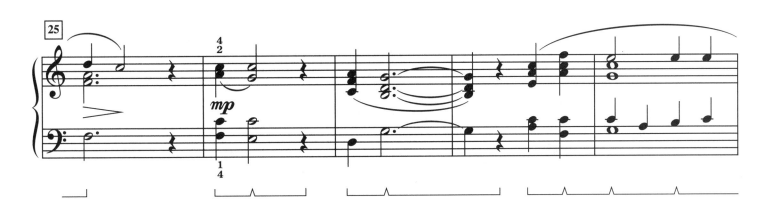

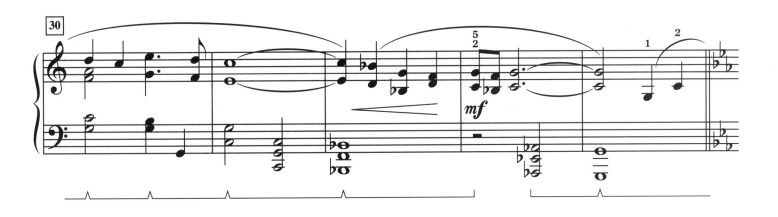

HALLELUJAH! WHAT A SAVIOR

Philip P. Bliss
Arr. Cindy Berry

WHEN I SURVEY THE WONDROUS CROSS

Lowell Mason
Arr. Cindy Berry

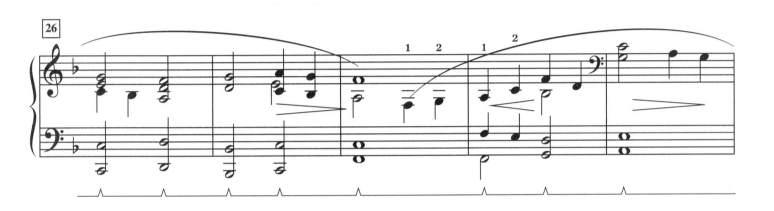

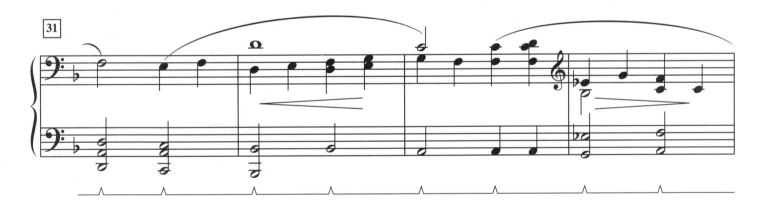

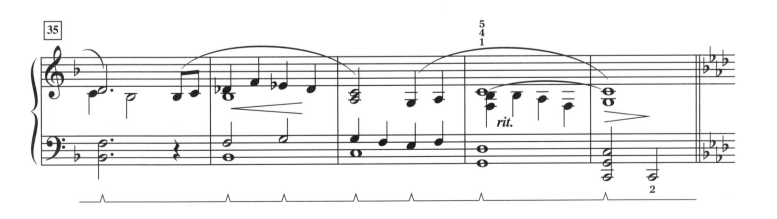

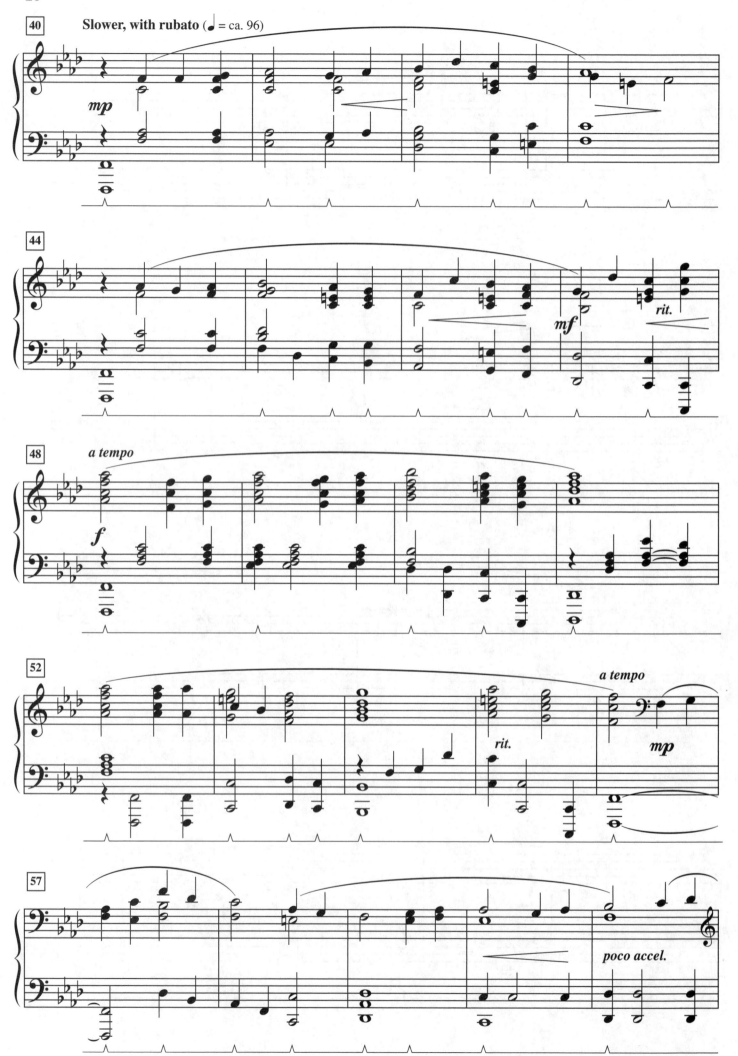

THE STRIFE IS O'ER, THE BATTLE DONE

Giovanni da Palestrina
Arr. Cindy Berry

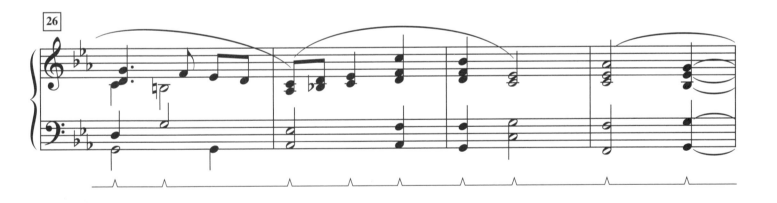

JUST AS I AM, WITHOUT ONE PLEA

William Bradbury
Arr. Cindy Berry

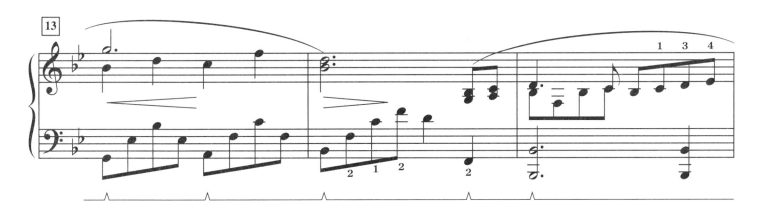

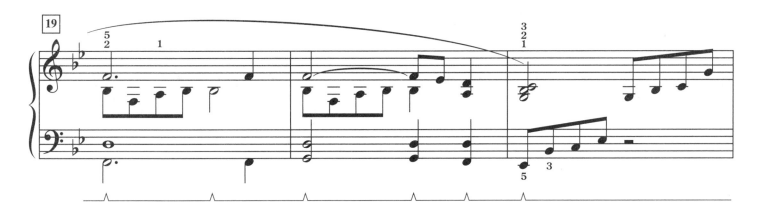

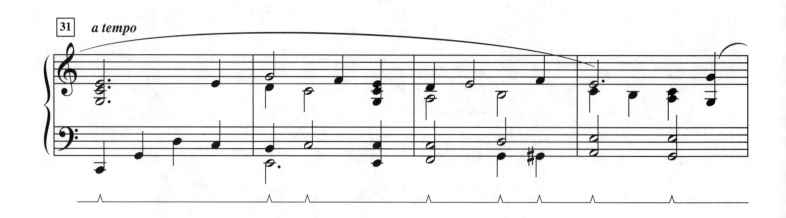

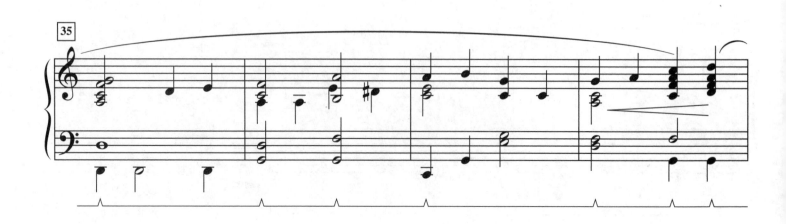

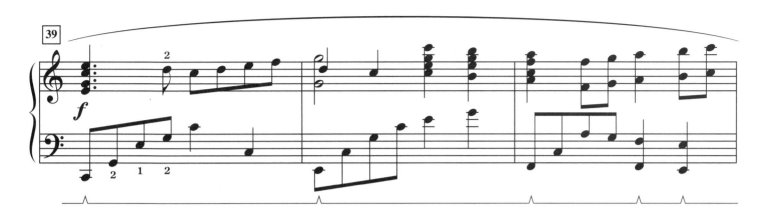

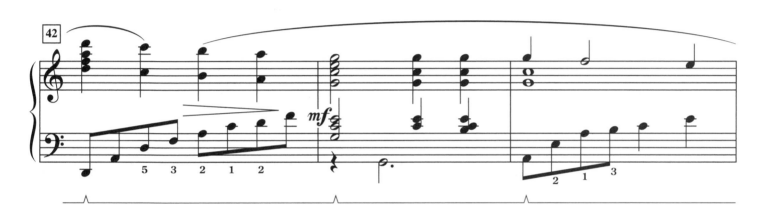

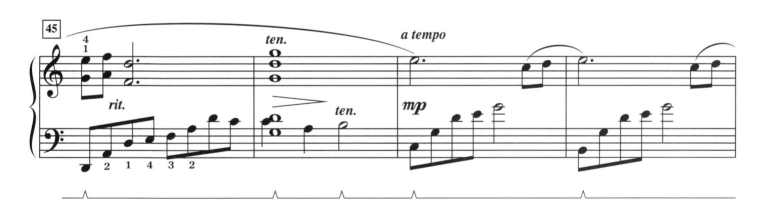

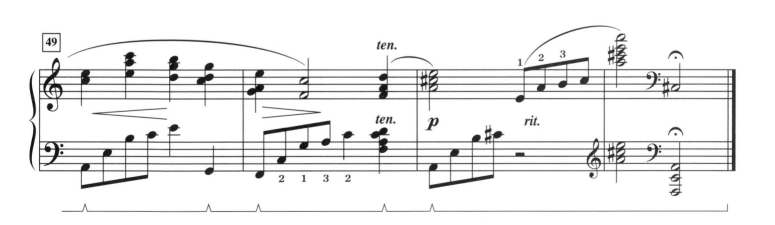

MY FAITH LOOKS UP TO THEE

Lowell Mason
Arr. Cindy Berry

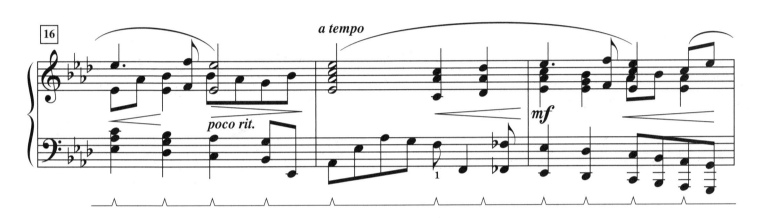

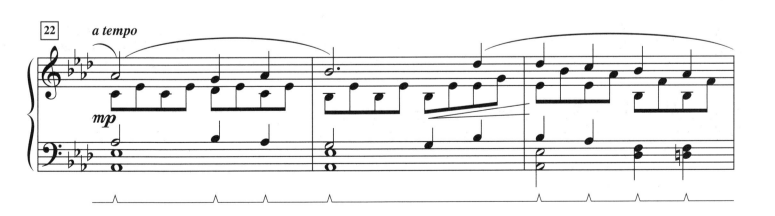